HOOFBEATS, CLAWS & RIPPLED FINS: CREATURE POEMS

Edited by

LEE BENNETT HOPKINS

Art by

STEPHEN ALCORN

To—
Pat Barbieri
and
Laura Pastore—
creature-lovers
—L.B.H.

For Ludovica
—S.A.

Text copyright © 2002 by Lee Bennett Hopkins

Illustrations copyright © 2002 by Stephen Alcorn

Page 32 represents an extension of the copyright page.

Printed in Hong Kong. All rights reserved.

www.harperchildrens.com

Library of Congress Cataloging-in-Publication Data

Hoofbeats, claws & rippled fins : creature poems / edited by Lee Bennett Hopkins ; art by
Stephen Alcorn.

    p.   cm.

  ISBN 0-688-17942-8 — ISBN 0-688-17943-6 (lib.bdg.)

  1. Animals—Juvenile poetry. 2. Children's poetry, American. [1. Animals—Poetry. 2.
American poetry—Collections.] I. Hopkins, Lee Bennett. II. Alcorn, Stephen, ill.

PS595.A5 H66 2002

811.008'0362—dc21   2001024018

Typography by Robbin Gourley

1 2 3 4 5 6 7 8 9 10

❖

First Edition

CONTENTS

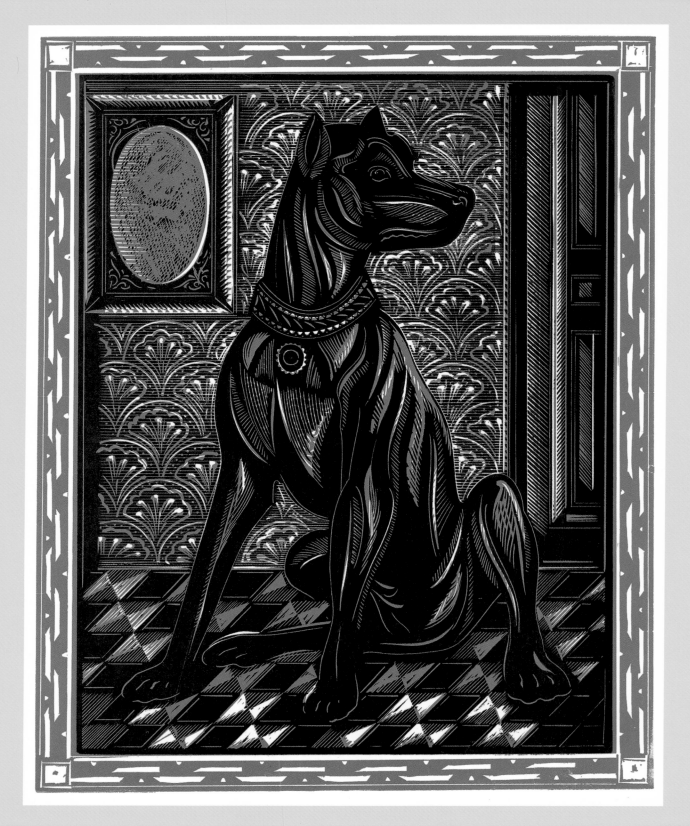

RUBY

LEE BENNETT HOPKINS

Welcoming
poets' poems
I—
with
my
muscular power
strong weight
nobility—

will not
hesitate
to let
you
in.

But
only
if you
come
gently,
quietly
through this
slightly opened
door

with
one
longed-for
biscuit

to toss
onto
my
royal floor.

IN AND OUT
KARLA KUSKIN

When she's in

she meows to be out.
When she's out
she meows to be in.

Whatever wherever whichever
however forever moreover
from cover to cover
from house mat to clover
she makes it quite clear
she would rather be here

if she's there.

If she's here

she would like to be there.
She would much rather far

if she's near
and near

if she's anywhere far.

Her preference is whimsical

wide and far-ranging.

Well what's a mind for
if it isn't for changing?

ROOSTER
RALPH FLETCHER

He looks like a dandy,
thrusting out his chest,
a swaggering boxer,
a henhouse tough guy,
strutting and preening

like a great poem
that knows who is
cock of the walk,
king of the collection.

He is loving and loyal,
standing on guard,
ready to rain terror
on any weasel or snake
who dares to disturb
the peace of his flock.

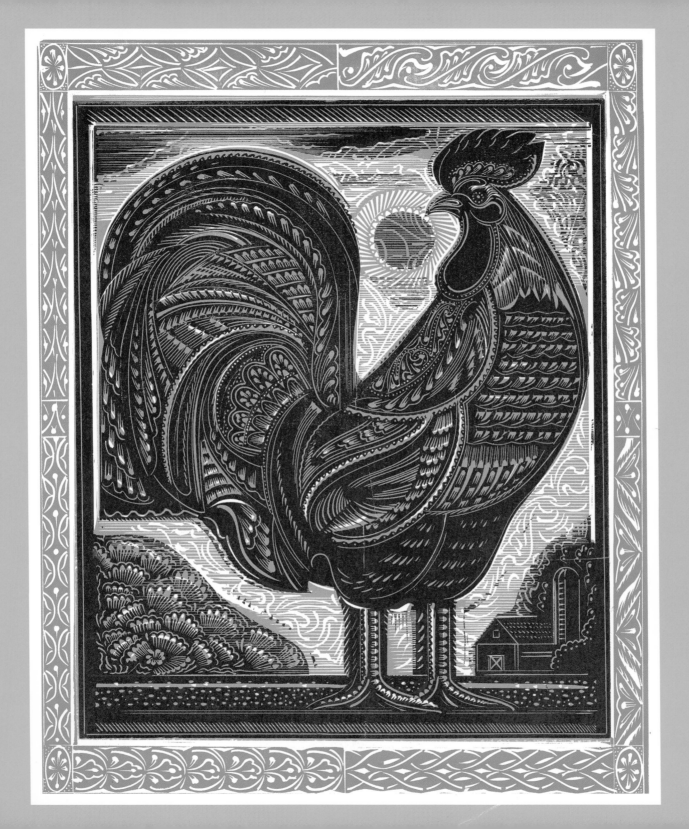

NIGHT HUNTER
PRINCE REDCLOUD

Strength
fills my
whiskered jaws

my powerful
mighty
razor-sharp
claws

I prowl
I stride
with silent feet

I need to eat

Take warning

Don't pause

not for
a
shadowed second
because . . .

because . . .

HERE'S FROG

KRISTINE O'CONNELL GEORGE

I.

Here's Frog, looking stuck
like a stubborn suction cup,
pebbled blob, a rippled pod,
just a lump of tucked-in frog.

Rubbered rock, he squats, dawdles,
ponders: *Short haul hop? Waddle?*
A moment of soggy contemplation
on froggy modes of transportation.

II.

Here's Frog, poker-faced,
looking immobile, sedate,
while plotting with smug delight
a brief amphibious flight—

blue under his belly, toes trailing
frog-in-the-sky, breathless, sailing,
the unleashing of hidden springs,
his whole self stretching, thinning,

as if His Frogginess had wings.

III.

Here's Frog, gathering in
almost . . . ready . . . to

LEAP again.

EASY LIVING
BEVERLY McLOUGHLAND

A cow
Takes life at ease.
She's more than pleased
To graze all day.
She's fond of clover,
Grass, and hay.
Her broomlike tail
Sweeps flies away.

A cow
Takes life in stride
She sits serenely
Side by side
With all her sister-cows.
She'll chew and chew,
And make good milk
And have a moo.

And more than that
She will not do.

14

IGUANA

TONY JOHNSTON

This swarthy being grazes the edges of dawn and dusk, so small under the ample gaze of sun and moon. He is humble as a glaze of mud, but he can praise the earth as well as anyone.

SHE LIKES TO HIDE

JANET S. WONG

She likes to hide in seaweed so much she has become it, inside and out, the ripple of her fins, the slippery touch of her skin, the veins between her scales.

When sun shines in the kelp forest, there she is at the beginning of time.

It is not about snails that crawl in her harbor. It is not about scum that floats its film on her eyes.

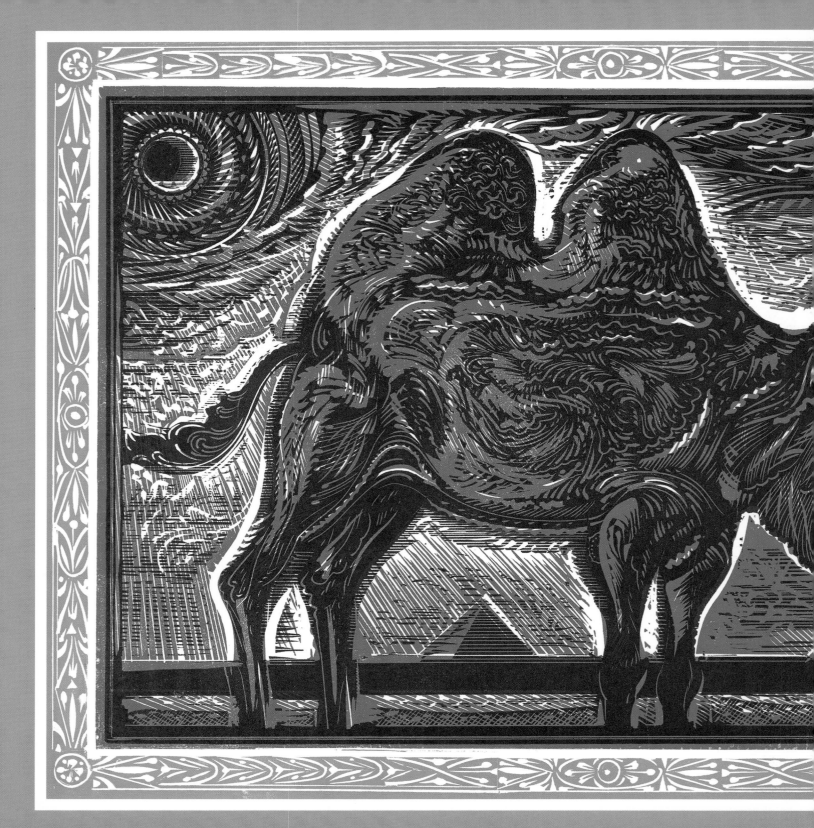

CAMEL
LILLIAN M. FISHER

A camel is a mammal,
A most extraordinary animal
Whose appearance is a wee bit odd.
His body is lumpy,
Knees calloused and bumpy,
And his feet are naturally shod.
His humps are fantastical,
His manner bombastical,
Due to his proud ancient past.
He feasts upon brambles
And ploddingly ambles.
His gait is not very fast.
But he carries great loads
On long dusty roads
Where many a beast cannot.
He's a tireless walker
And goes without water
In weather increasingly hot.
This strange-looking beast
Who resides in the East
And in far-off places West
Is found at the zoo
Where he's happy, it's true,
But—
Deep inside—desert is best.

TRIASSIC TRIUMPH
AVIS HARLEY

Reptile eye
shining inside its leather cave
measures
the heavy afternoon.

Eons ago
Turtle left the starting gate,
not even knowing the word
late.

Clad only in her bony home
and steady as a metronome,
she plods past dinosaurs,
predators,
a snoozing rabbit fool—
barely beating out
the carver's tool.

Click-clack click-clack down the track
laden with legends upon her back;

Old Slow Toes holds her place
in this great enduring race.

ANTEATER
ALICE SCHERTLE

Too late

You turned the page too late
to see them

three scouts
each no larger than a semicolon;

two almost hidden in the crack of the gutter

one more running along a sentence

You know how it is

first three

then hordes   dark streams down the page

The scouts
are only the vanguard

Never mind

He saw them

PORCUPINE
REBECCA KAI DOTLICH

Bedazzled by bristles,
bewhiskered with points,
lumbering
on clumsy joints—
shuffling along
knobby branch of pine;
rattling quills
along his spine,

He nestles into
branch of chair;
settles down
to evening air—
tightly tucked
and in between
shade of spruce;
sweet evergreen,

Quiet prince of timber, he
needles into limb
and tree;
claims this place—
ah, forest throne,
to wind and woodlands
he calls home.

BUFFALO
JOSEPH BRUCHAC

One bull Buffalo, standing alone,
turns his great head to face the storm.
His muscles ripple with lazy strength.
Even the grizzlies, lords of the mountains,
turn away when Buffalo lowers his horns.

The Plains nations praised Buffalo.
Lakota, Mandan, Cheyenne, Crow,
Kiowa, Pueblo, Arapaho.

His meat was their food.
His hide covered tipis.
His sinews strung their hunting bows.

His great herds flowed
through the heart of this land.
Shaggy rivers of thunder rumbled the plains.
Dust from Buffalo's passing darkened sun
before the coming of men with guns.

His dark eyes tell the story.
Many died, but Buffalo survived.

Here and there on wide parklands,
if you are quiet as you go
you may stand close, feel the ancient power
hear the hoofbeat song of Buffalo.

FULL MOON AND OWL
ANN WHITFORD PAUL

Full Moon and Owl together stare,

three round eyes watching night.

Moon's white shines a friendly glare.

Full Moon and Owl together stare.

But Owl's cold gold warns *Beware*

and all small creatures quake with fright.

Full Moon and Owl together stare,

three round eyes watching night.

ACKNOWLEDGMENTS

Thanks are due to the following for use of works especially
commissioned for this collection:

Curtis Brown, Ltd., for "Porcupine" by Rebecca Kai Dotlich,
copyright © 2002 by Rebecca Kai Dotlich. "Ruby" by Lee Bennett Hopkins,
copyright © 2002 by Lee Bennett Hopkins. "Night Hunter" by
Prince Redcloud, copyright © 2002 by Prince Redcloud.
All printed by permission of Curtis Brown, Ltd.

Marian Reiner for "Rooster" by Ralph Fletcher, copyright © 2002 by
Ralph Fletcher. Used by permission of Marian Reiner for the author.

All other works used by permission of the respective poets, each of
whom controls all rights.